MW00973992

Georgia
Bulldogs
TRIVIA CHALLENGE

SOURCEBOOKS, INC.®
NAPERVILLE, ILLINOIS

Published by Sourcebooks, Inc.
P.O. Box 4410, Naperville, Illinois 60567-4410
(630) 961-3900
Fax: (630) 961-2168
www.sourcebooks.com

Printed and bound in Canada
WC 10 9 8 7 6 5 4 3 2

The University of Georgia has produced some of the most recognizable names in college football, from Vince Dooley and Herschel Walker, to Uga the V and VI. The Bulldog tradition, one of the oldest and most storied in the South, includes both national championships and Heisman Trophy winners—a combination even rivals Alabama and Tennessee can't claim. Georgia has yielded NFL MVPs, Super Bowl winners, and inductees into both the College and Pro Football Halls of Fame. And then there are the NCAA records, school milestones, and classic bowl games—all of which have run side-by-side throughout Georgia history with some of the most colorful characters in the game.

These 200 questions should test your knowledge of all of it, from all-time rushing records to once-in-a-lifetime game-winning plays. From the quirky early coaches to the game-day traditions cooked up by the crowd. If you're both a stat geek and a passionate fan, you should be able to get to the last page without clicking on your browser or calling a classmate. The questions and topics are designed to grow tougher, taking you from the big records and names to the obscure and bizarre. Get half of the answers right, and Vince Dooley would probably still be proud!

THE MARK RICHT ERA

1. **Which season did Mark Richt become Georgia's head coach?**
   - a. 2003
   - b. 2001
   - c. 1999
   - d. 1997

2. **Richt came to Georgia from what job?**
   - a. Florida State offensive coordinator
   - b. Florida State receivers coach
   - c. Florida offensive coordinator
   - d. Miami offensive coordinator

3. **How many years had Richt spent at that previous school?**
   - a. 1
   - b. 5
   - c. 8
   - d. 15

4. **Mark Richt played football for which university?**
   - a. Miami
   - b. The Citadel
   - c. Tennessee
   - d. Troy State

5. **Richt became the _____ head football coach in Georgia history.**

   a. 15th
   b. 20th
   c. 25th
   d. 30th

6. **As a quarterbacks coach earlier in his career, Richt worked with which two Heisman Trophy winners?**

   a. Charlie Ward and Chris Weinke
   b. Gino Torretta and Vinny Testaverde
   c. Chris Weinke and Danny Wuerffel
   d. Charlie Ward and Danny Wuerffel

7. **Which quarterback is also Richt's brother-in-law?**

   a. Chris Weinke
   b. Danny Wuerffel
   c. Casey Weldon
   d. Brad Johnson

8. **Where is Richt originally from?**

   a. Miami
   b. Atlanta
   c. Omaha
   d. Kansas City

9. **The 2007 Bulldog team won the last _____ games of the season.**

   a. 6
   b. 7
   c. 8
   d. 9

10. **Georgia won an SEC championship in 2002 for the first time in _____ years.**

    a. 10
    b. 15
    c. 20
    d. 25

11. What team did the Bulldogs defeat in the Sugar Bowl at the end of that season?

a. Miami
b. Florida State
c. Michigan
d. Virginia Tech

12. After the 2007 season, where did Georgia finish in the Associated Press poll?

a. 2nd
b. 5th
c. 8th
d. 11th

13. In Mark Richt's first seven seasons, through 2007, how many bowl games have the Bulldogs been to?

a. 4
b. 5
c. 6
d. 7

TRADITIONS

14. **The mascot for Georgia's first ever game was a
    _____.**

    a. goat
    b. dog
    c. falcon
    d. mule

15. **The first dog mascot in 1894 for Georgia was a
    _____.**

    a. bulldog
    b. border collie
    c. beagle
    d. bull terrier

16. **Each of Georgia's Uga mascots receives a _____.**

    a. retirement party
    b. honorary degree
    c. varsity letter
    d. special jersey

17. **The biggest of all the Uga mascots was Uga VI. How
    much did he weigh?**

    a. 50 lbs
    b. 55 lbs
    c. 60 lbs
    d. 65 lbs

18. The Georgia band is known as the _____.

a. Redcoat Band
b. Bulldog Band
c. Georgia Red
d. Pride of the South

19. Who was responsible for redesigning the Georgia "G" on the team's football helmets?

a. Vince Lombardi
b. Vince Dooley
c. Herschel Walker
d. Mark Richt

20. Georgia sought permission from whom to use that redesigned "G"?

a. the New York Giants
b. the PGA Tour
c. the Green Bay Packers
d. Georgia Tech

21. Many Georgia faithfuls believe that the nickname Bulldogs came from _____ because the first University of Georgia president was a graduate of the Ivy League school.

a. Harvard
b. Brown
c. Columbia
d. Yale

22. In a 1920 article in the *Atlanta Journal Constitution*, sportswriter Morgan Blake advocated the nickname Bulldogs, saying "the Georgia Bulldogs would sound good because _____."

a. there is a certain dignity about a bulldog, as well as ferocity
b. there is no shame in taking another school's nickname
c. in nature, a bulldog would stand a pretty good chance of taking down a gator
d. labradors, beagles, poodles, or Dalmatians just won't do

23. Uga V was also seen _____.

a. on a box of Wheaties
b. on the cover of *Sports Illustrated*
c. on his own trading card
d. on a series of dog food commercials

24. As of the 2007 season, what is the name of the most current mascot?

a. Uga IV
b. Uga V
c. Uga VI
d. Uga VII

25. What did Uga VI do to commemorate Vince Dooley's last game as Georgia athletic director in 2003?

a. He presented Dooley with a rose in a pre-game ceremony.
b. He wore a black jersey, instead of his typical red.
c. He fetched a football thrown by Dooley in a pre-game ceremony.
d. He was officially renamed "Uga Dooley."

26. For more than 50 years, Ugas have come from a family in what Georgia town?

a. Atlanta
b. Athens
c. Savannah
d. Augusta

27. Georgia is the only major college in the country that _____.

a. has a live animal for a mascot
b. buries its mascots inside the stadium
c. assigns its mascot an official roster number
d. actually enrolls its mascot with the university registrar

28. Georgia famously wears _____.

a. silver britches
b. golden cleats
c. bronze helmets
d. black sleeves

29. What is the name of Georgia's fight song?

a. "Fight, Georgia, Fight!"
b. "The Bulldog Ballad"
c. "Ol' U-G-A"
d. "Glory, Glory"

30. It is sung to the tune of what song?

a. "The Battle Hymn of the Republic"
b. "I've Been Working on the Railroad"
c. "Georgia on My Mind"
d. "She'll be Comin' Round the Mountain"

31. What campus tradition commemorates each Georgia victory?

a. The clock tower is lit.
b. The chapel bell is rung.
c. Fireworks are set off.
d. The band holds a vigil.

32. Overeager fans broke the 877-pound chapel bell in 2007 after a victory over which opponent?

a. Florida
b. Tennessee
c. Alabama
d. LSU

33. Uga V appeared in which movie?

a. *Midnight in the Garden of Good and Evil*
b. *Men in Black*
c. *Pearl Harbor*
d. *Tommy Boy*

HERSCHEL WALKER

34. Walker holds the NCAA record for _____.

a. most yards rushing in a career
b. most yards rushing in a three-year stretch
c. career rushing touchdowns
d. most yards gained in a single game

35. Herschel Walker's number _____ is now retired at Georgia.

a. 12
b. 21
c. 34
d. 40

36. Where in Georgia did Walker grow up?

a. Cartersville
b. Wrightsville
c. Thomasville
d. Clarkesville

37. Which year did Walker win the Heisman?

a. 1980
b. 1981
c. 1982
d. 1983

38. How many times in his career did Walker finish in the top three in Heisman balloting?

a. 1
b. 2
c. 3
d. 4

39. Walker set the NCAA freshman rushing record with how many yards?

a. 911
b. 1,232
c. 1,616
d. 2,122

40. As of 2008, Walker still holds the single-season Georgia rushing record with how many yards?

a. 1,001
b. 1,359
c. 1,891
d. 2,012

41. He also holds the single-game school rushing record with how many yards?

a. 189
b. 283
c. 332
d. 359

42. How many rushing touchdowns did Walker have in his career?

a. 29
b. 35
c. 49
d. 58

43 How many times during the 1981 season did Herschel Walker gain at least 100 yards?

a. 8
b. 9
c. 10
d. 11

44. How many times did Walker gain more than 200 yards or more during his career?

    a. 7

    b. 8

    c. 9

    d. 10

45. What was Georgia's record during Herschel Walker's tenure?

    a. 34–0

    b. 32–2

    c. 29–5

    d. 25–9

46. Which was NOT one of the teams Walker later played for in the NFL?

    a. the New York Giants

    b. the Philadelphia Eagles

    c. the Minnesota Vikings

    d. the Detroit Lions

47. Why did Walker sign out of college with the USFL instead of the NFL?

    a. The USFL offered him a $1 million signing bonus.

    b. Walker said he would rather be "the first star in a new league than just another star in the NFL."

    c. He would have had to wait another year to be eligible for the NFL draft.

    d. Donald Trump, a USFL owner, personally wooed him to join the league.

48. Which team did he sign with out of Georgia?

    a. the Birmingham Stallions

    b. the Michigan Panthers

    c. the San Antonio Gunslingers

    d. the New Jersey Generals

49. **Which two quarterbacks and future NFL stars did Walker beat for the Heisman that season?**

a. John Elway and Dan Marino
b. Jim McMahon and Doug Flutie
c. Boomer Esiason and Vinny Testaverde
d. Bernie Kosar and Jeff Hostettler

50. **In 1989, the Dallas Cowboys famously did what with Herschel Walker?**

a. acquired him in the 5th round of the NFL draft
b. replaced him in the starting lineup with Emmitt Smith
c. used him in a disastrously unpopular advertising campaign
d. traded him to Minnesota for five players and six draft picks

SANFORD STADIUM

51. As of 2008, Sanford Stadium ranks as the fifth-largest on-campus stadium in the nation with what capacity?

a. 88,746
b. 92,746
c. 97,746
d. 101,746

52. Who is S.V. Sanford, the stadium's namesake?

a. an early Georgia head coach
b. a former UGA president
c. a former U.S. Senator from Georgia
d. Georgia's biggest booster during the 1970s

53. Games were first played in the stadium in which year?

a. 1919
b. 1929
c. 1937
d. 1948

54. Who was Georgia's first opponent in the newly opened stadium?

a. Georgia Tech
b. Florida
c. Yale
d. Duke

55. What was the original cost of constructing the stadium?

a. $3,600
b. $36,000
c. $360,000
d. $3.6 million

56. **The game against Kentucky on October 26, 1940, was the first _____ at Sanford Stadium.**
   a. sell-out
   b. televised game
   c. SEC game
   d. night game

57. **During the 1996 Olympics, Sanford Stadium played host to what events?**
   a. all of the track and field events
   b. the start and finish of the marathon
   c. the women's softball games
   d. the men's and women's soccer games

58. **What is Georgia's longest winning streak, as of 2008, at Sanford Stadium?**
   a. 15 games
   b. 24 games
   c. 32 games
   d. 40 games

59. **What is the only SEC school with a larger stadium capacity than Georgia's, as of 2008?**
   a. Florida
   b. Alabama
   c. Auburn
   d. Tennessee

60. **What is the current playing surface at Sanford Stadium?**
   a. natural grass
   b. Astroturf
   c. natural grass on the playing field and artificial turf on the sidelines
   d. synthetic Bermudagrass

61. **Games at Georgia are often said to be played _____.**
   a. on the hill
   b. inside the gates
   c. between the hedges
   d. under the ropes

CONFERENCE PLAY

62. Which division of the SEC does Georgia play in?

   a. Northern
   b. Southern
   c. Eastern
   d. Western

63. What was the first conference Georgia joined?

   a. the Georgia Intercollegiate Athletic Conference
   b. the Southern Conference
   c. the Southern Intercollegiate Athletic Association
   d. the Southern Alliance of Independent Schools

64. Which year did Georgia win its first conference title?

   a. 1912
   b. 1920
   c. 1934
   d. 1941

65. Which year did Georgia later begin competition as a charter member of SEC?

   a. 1917
   b. 1924
   c. 1933
   d. 1940

66. **All but three of the charter members of the SEC, along with Georgia, are still in the conference today. What are the three schools that no longer participate?**

   a. Georgia Tech, Sewanee, and Tulane
   b. Florida State, Georgia Tech, and North Carolina
   c. Memphis, East Carolina, and UAB
   d. Rice, Louisiana-Monroe, and Jacksonville University

67. **Which postseason bowl games have been affiliated with automatic tie-ins to the SEC?**

   a. the Independence Bowl, the Music City Bowl, and the Liberty Bowl
   b. the Meineke Car Care Bowl, the Alamo Bowl, and the Sun Bowl
   c. the Emerald Bowl, the Poinsettia Bowl, and the Las Vegas Bowl
   d. the Gator Bowl, the Armed Forces Bowl, and the Humanitarian Bowl

68. **During which stretch did the Bulldogs win three straight SEC championships?**

   a. 1968–70
   b. 1974–76
   c. 1980–82
   d. 2003–05

69. **Georgia played in its first SEC championship game in 2002 and defeated which opponent?**

   a. Arkansas
   b. Alabama
   c. Auburn
   d. LSU

70. **The SEC today spans schools in how many different states?**

   a. 6
   b. 7
   c. 8
   d. 9

71. Georgia shares a division in the SEC with which other schools?

a. Alabama, Auburn, and Arkansas
b. South Carolina, Ole Miss, and Mississippi State
c. Florida, LSU, and South Carolina
d. Kentucky, Tennessee, and Vanderbilt

72. Eric Zeier's SEC record for career passing yards (11,153) was later broken by which quarterback?

a. Peyton Manning
b. Danny Wuerffel
c. JaMarcus Russell
d. Rex Grossman

73. Georgia ran the ball 89 times, an SEC record, against which opponent in 1967?

a. Kentucky
b. South Carolina
c. Florida
d. Georgia Tech

NATIONAL CHAMPIONSHIPS

74. In addition to Georgia's two consensus national championships, the Bulldogs have won how many other national titles, as recognized by various polling services over the years?

    a. 2
    b. 3
    c. 4
    d. 5

75. Georgia recognizes the school's first national championship as having come in what year?

    a. 1916
    b. 1927
    c. 1942
    d. 1946

76. What year was Georgia's first consensus national championship?

    a. 1942
    b. 1946
    c. 1968
    d. 1976

77. Who did the Bulldogs defeat in the Rose Bowl at the end of that season?

    a. USC
    b. Michigan
    c. Ohio State
    d. UCLA

78. **Georgia's only loss during the regular season that year was to which team?**
   a. Georgia Tech
   b. Auburn
   c. Florida
   d. Alabama

79. **Who did the Bulldogs defeat in the Sugar Bowl at the end of the 1980 national championship season?**
   a. Michigan
   b. Texas
   c. Ohio State
   d. Notre Dame

80. **That game was the first-ever _____.**
   a. meeting of Georgia and Notre Dame
   b. national championship played under the Bowl Alliance system
   c. championship game nationally televised
   d. national championship game played in the Super Dome

81. **Who was named the MVP of that game?**
   a. Terry Hoage
   b. Rex Robinson
   c. Buck Belue
   d. Herschel Walker

82. **Which Bulldog had two interceptions in that game, including one late in the game on a 4th-and-1 Notre Dame desperation pass?**
   a. Terry Hoage
   b. Scott Woerner
   c. Mike Fisher
   d. Chris Welton

83. **Georgia lost a potential second national championship in three seasons with a loss to which team in the Sugar Bowl at the end of the 1982 season?**
   a. Nebraska
   b. UCLA
   c. Southern Methodist
   d. Penn State

VINCE DOOLEY

84. Which season did Vince Dooley arrive?

    a. 1958
    b. 1964
    c. 1970
    d. 1974

85. How many games did Dooley win at Georgia in 25 seasons?

    a. 101
    b. 151
    c. 201
    d. 251

86. Dooley remained at Georgia in what position, until 2004, after retiring as football coach?

    a. university trustee
    b. special advisor to the athletic director
    c. athletic director
    d. honorary football coach

87. How many SEC titles did Georgia win during Dooley's coaching tenure?

    a. 5
    b. 6
    c. 7
    d. 8

88. Dooley played college football for which university?

a. Auburn
b. Georgia
c. Georgia Tech
d. Alabama

89. Dooley also was a head coach at what other university in his career?

a. Auburn
b. Georgia Southern
c. Furman
d. nowhere else

90. Dooley coached against his brother, Bill, in the 1971 Gator Bowl while Bill was the head coach at what university?

a. Auburn
b. Wake Forest
c. North Carolina
d. Virginia Tech

91. As of 2008, only one coach in SEC history has ever won more games at a single school than Vince Dooley did. Who is the other coach?

a. Tennessee's Gen. Robert Neyland
b. Alabama's Bear Bryant
c. Auburn's Shug Jordan
d. Florida's Steve Spurrier

92. Which was NOT one of the years Georgia won an SEC championship under Dooley?

a. 1968
b. 1972
c. 1976
d. 1980

93. In Vince Dooley's 25 seasons as Georgia's head coach, how many bowls did he take the Bulldogs to?

a. 24
b. 20
c. 16
d. 13

94. What happened during Dooley's final season as head coach in 1988?

a. The Bulldogs won their second national championship under him.
b. Georgia had a losing record for the first time in Dooley's tenure.
c. The Bulldogs won the last of their SEC championships under Dooley.
d. Georgia went 9–3 and won Dooley's last game in the Gator Bowl.

HONORS AND AWARDS

95. Which of the following is **NOT** an all-star game that Georgia players have participated in over the years?

a. the Blue-Gray Game
b. the Gridiron Classic
c. the Japan Bowl
d. the North–South Game

96. As of 2008, how many jersey numbers has Georgia retired?

a. 1
b. 2
c. 4
d. 6

97. The number 62 was retired in which player's honor?

a. Charley Trippi
b. Frank Sinkwich
c. Theron Sapp
d. Garrison Hearst

98. As of 2008, who are Georgia's two Heisman Trophy winners?

a. Herschel Walker and Charley Trippi
b. Herschel Walker and Garrison Hearst
c. Charley Trippi and Theron Sapp
d. Herschel Walker and Frank Sinkwich

99. **Charley Trippi was a runner-up in the 1946 Heisman Trophy balloting to which winner?**
   a. Notre Dame's John Lujack
   b. Army's Glenn Davis
   c. Army's Doc Blanchard
   d. Southern Methodist's Doak Walker

100. **Which Georgia player, in 1983, became the highest-finishing defensive back ever in Heisman Trophy voting, at 5th?**
   a. Terry Hoage
   b. Scott Woerner
   c. Bill Krug
   d. Jeff Sanchez

101. **Who was Georgia's first All-American?**
   a. Herb Maffett
   b. Tom Nash
   c. David Paddock
   d. Bob McWhorter

102. **Why did guard Ralph Maddox NOT become an All-American until 32 years after his Georgia career had ended?**
   a. The honor was bestowed retroactively when additional statistics were later uncovered.
   b. His International News Service honor had never been recorded and was only later uncovered.
   c. The International News Service honored him later as one of its "All-Americans of the Century."
   d. Maddox had initially refused the honor and it was only posthumously accepted by his son.

103. **Why did Maddox never learn of this?**
   a. The university kept the information a secret until Maddox's death, at his children's request.
   b. The honor wasn't awarded until after his death.
   c. He was killed in World War II before the university discovered the honor.
   d. He died in an airplane crash a year after his Georgia career ended.

104. What honor did end George Poschner earn after his Georgia career?

a. induction into the Pro Football Hall of Fame
b. a Blue-Gray game MVP
c. a Super Bowl ring
d. a Purple Heart

105. As of 2008, who are the only two Georgia players in both the College and Pro Football Halls of Fame?

a. John Rauch and Fran Tarkenton
b. Charley Trippi and Catfish Smith
c. Charley Trippi and Fran Tarkenton
d. John Rauch and Herschel Walker

106. Which two pairs of brothers were both named All-Americans at Georgia?

a. Champ and Boss Bailey; Matt and Jon Stinchcomb
b. Ronald and Champ Bailey; Ray and Scott Rissmiller
c. Dan and Dale Edwards; Harry and Steve Babcock
d. Jim and Dave Wilson; Craig and William Hertwig

107. Georgia has had two three-time All-America first-team players. Herschel Walker is one; who is the other?

a. Matt Stinchcomb
b. Terry Hoage
c. David Pollack
d. Pat Dye

HISTORY

108. **Which year did Georgia first begin playing football?**

- a. 1888
- b. 1892
- c. 1894
- d. 1900

109. **That year, Georgia and which opponent inaugurated what would become the oldest football rivalry in the South?**

- a. Auburn
- b. Alabama
- c. Tennessee
- d. Georgia Tech

110. **Who was Georgia's first football game played against?**

- a. Georgia Tech
- b. Vanderbilt
- c. Furman
- d. Mercer

111. **Who was Georgia's first football coach?**

- a. Billy Reynolds
- b. Charles McCarthy
- c. Charles Herty
- d. J. Coulter

112. **What other job did that coach hold at the university?**

a. president
b. chemistry professor
c. English department chair
d. student health services director

113. **What fundamental change occurred at Georgia and throughout college football in 1906?**

a. Helmets were required for the first time.
b. The NCAA was created.
c. The forward pass was legalized.
d. The length of the field was made uniform at 100 yards.

114. **Georgia did NOT play football during which seasons because of war?**

a. 1918 and 1943
b. 1917 and 1918
c. 1942 and 1943
d. 1942–1945

115. **The 1927 Bulldogs, who went 9–1, were called the _____ team.**

a. "dream and wonder"
b. "divide and conquer"
c. "razzle and dazzle"
d. "run and gun"

116. **Which Bulldog won the 1968 Outland Trophy, given to college football's top interior lineman?**

a. Bill Stanfill
b. Steve Greer
c. George Patton
d. Jim Wilson

117. In which decade did the Bulldogs record the most victories, with 89 wins?

a. 1940s
b. 1970s
c. 1980s
d. 1990s

118. As of 2008, when was the last time Georgia went undefeated in a season?

a. 2002
b. 1982
c. 1980
d. 1946

119. Entering the 2008 season, when was the last time Georgia was ranked No. 1 in the nation in the Associated Press poll?

a. early in the 2004 season
b. near the end of the 2002 season
c. late in the 1982 season
d. at the end of the 1980 season

MEMORABLE PLAYERS

120. What was Vernon Smith's nickname?

a. "Catfish"
b. "Crawfish"
c. "Trout"
d. "Snapper"

121. What did Frank Sinkwich do later in life?

a. He returned to Georgia as the head football coach.
b. He was elected to the U.S. Senate from Georgia.
c. He opened a chain of popular restaurants in Athens.
d. He became a wholesale beer distributor.

122. Theron Sapp earned what nickname for scoring the lone touchdown in Georgia's 7–0 1957 victory over Georgia Tech, snapping an eight-year losing streak to the in-state rivals?

a. The Bee Keeper
b. The Streak Snapper
c. The Drought Breaker
d. The Rain Maker

123. All-American safety Lynn Hughes originally played what position at Georgia?

a. quarterback
b. nose tackle
c. wide receiver
d. kicker

124. **Multi-talented All-American tackle Ray Rissmiller later produced _____.**

   a. a book, *Big Ray*, about his Georgia playing days
   b. a single, "Big Ray," with a recording company
   c. a documentary, *Big Ray*, about college linemen
   d. a painting, "Big Ray," that sold at auction for $23,000

125. **Charley Trippi's Georgia career was interrupted for more than two years because _____.**

   a. of service in World War II
   b. of a severely fractured right leg
   c. of academic ineligibility
   d. Georgia halted its football program during the war

126. **Which Georgia quarterback did NOT wear the number 14 in Athens? (Hint: He wore #12.)**

   a. Mike Bobo
   b. David Greene
   c. Kirby Moore
   d. Zeke Bratkowski

127. **What number did Frank Sinkwich wear?**

   a. 1
   b. 21
   c. 42
   d. 48

128. **Bob McWhorter was the first Georgia athlete to _____.**

   a. be recruited out of high school
   b. captain both the football and basketball teams
   c. go on to sign a pro contract
   d. play both ways on the football field

129. What did the student body do for All-American quarterback David Paddock?

a. They elected him their president.
b. They voted him Georgia's all-time best athlete.
c. They circulated a petition requesting that he play for the football team.
d. They named the stadium student section after him.

130. All-American halfback John Bond later served in what capacity in World War II?

a. a surgeon
b. an undercover intelligence operative
c. a bomber pilot
d. submarine crewman

131. Where did Zeke Bratkowski grow up before attending UGA?

a. Iowa
b. Minnesota
c. Idaho
d. Illinois

132. In addition to football, All-American end Johnny Carson also lettered in three other sports at Georgia. Which of the following was NOT one of them?

a. golf
b. basketball
c. track
d. baseball

133. Georgia All-American guard Pat Dye later became the head football coach of which of the Bulldogs' rivals?

a. Alabama
b. Georgia Tech
c. Auburn
d. Florida

134. Which Georgia quarterback was home-grown in Athens?

a. David Greene
b. Fran Tarkenton
c. Mike Bobo
d. Johnny Rauch

135. What was All-American offensive tackle Mike Wilson's nickname?

a. "Mad dog"
b. "Moonpie"
c. "Meaty"
d. "Man-eater"

136. Future All-American offensive guard Joel Parrish arrived at Georgia after turning down _____.

a. a scholarship offer from Notre Dame
b. a professional contract with the Los Angeles Dodgers
c. an invitation to the 1976 Olympic Games
d. a basketball scholarship to Kentucky

BIG GAMES AND BOWLS

137. Georgia and Florida officials would like people to stop referring to the annual meeting of the two rivals in Jacksonville as _____.

a. "the world's largest outdoor cocktail party"
b. "the Beer Can Bowl"
c. "the world's greatest excuse to tailgate"
d. "the greatest drunken reunion in the South"

138. That game has been held in Jacksonville nearly every year since _____

a. 1982
b. 1968
c. 1946
d. 1933

139. Since then, it was moved out of town for a two-year stretch only once because of _____.

a. World War II
b. stadium construction with the arrival of the Jacksonville Jaguars
c. local complaints about noise and disturbance by rowdy fans
d. an ill-fated plan to play the game instead in Atlanta

140. In the two teams' meeting in that game in 2007, Florida quarterback and eventual Heisman Trophy winner Tim Tebow was sacked how many times?

a. 3
b. 4
c. 6
d. 7

141. Which two players accounted for all six of Georgia's touchdowns in that game?

a. Mikey Henderson and Knowshon Moreno
b. Mohamed Massaquoi and Brannan Southerland
c. Matthew Stafford and Mohamed Massaquoi
d. Knowshon Moreno and Matthew Stafford

142. What was the first bowl game Georgia ever played in, in 1942?

a. the Cotton Bowl
b. the Gator Bowl
c. the Sugar Bowl
d. the Orange Bowl

143. Which of the following is NOT a bowl game Georgia has ever played in?

a. the Oil Bowl
b. the O'ahu Bowl
c. the Grapefruit Bowl
d. the Tangerine Bowl

144. Which bowl game has Georgia played in more times than any other?

a. the Sugar Bowl
b. the Peach Bowl
c. the Cotton Bowl
d. the Gator Bowl

145. Who was on the receiving end of Charley Trippi's 67-yard touchdown pass in the 1947 Gator Bowl tie with Maryland?

a. Harry Babcock
b. Dan Edwards
c. Jim Campagna
d. Frank Sinkwich

146. Frank Sinkwich had what is considered one of the greatest performances ever in the _____ Bowl, where in 1942 he passed for 243 yards and three touchdowns and ran for another 139 yards and one touchdown.

a. Orange
b. Sugar
c. Rose
d. Cotton

147. Defensive tackle George Patton got to fulfill his dream of playing what position in the 1966 Cotton Bowl?

a. running back
b. wide receiver
c. quarterback
d. kicker

148. Who kicked the winning field goal in the rain with 9 seconds to play to break a 10–10 tie with Georgia Tech in the final regular-season game of the 1976 season?

a. Ben Zambiasi
b. Kevin Butler
c. Rex Robinson
d. Allan Leavitt

149. Which defensive back had two fourth-quarter interceptions to help Georgia defeat Clemson in 1985?

a. Terry Hoage
b. Tony Flack
c. John Little
d. Gary Moss

INDIVIDUAL RECORDS

150. **In the 1993 game against Southern Mississippi, Eric Zeier passed the ball 47 times for how many yards, a school record?**

   a. 344
   b. 444
   c. 544
   d. 644

151. **As a receiver, cornerback, and kick returner, Champ Bailey played more than _____ plays in the 1998 season alone.**

   a. 500
   b. 750
   c. 1,000
   d. 1,500

152. **Beginning in 1945, how many consecutive games did John Rauch start at quarterback for the Bulldogs?**

   a. 18
   b. 26
   c. 34
   d. 45

153. **Who holds the Georgia record for the longest rushing touchdown, at 89 yards?**

   a. Frank Harvey
   b. Tim Worley
   c. Dobby Dellinger
   d. James Ray

154. The Georgia record for the longest kickoff return for a touchdown, 99 yards, was set by which player?

a. Fred Gibson in 2002
b. Tim Worley in 1988
c. Thomas Brown in 2006
d. Lamar Davis in 1940

155. Which player holds the Georgia record for longest field goal, as of 2008?

a. Brandon Coutu in 2005
b. Kevin Butler in 1984
c. Billy Bennett in 2001
d. Durward Pennington in 1961

156. How long was it?

a. 54 yards
b. 57 yards
c. 60 yards
d. 63 yards

157. Which player ran back a punt return for a 100-yard touchdown?

a. Buzy Rosenberg in 1970
b. Johnny Cook in 1942
c. Mickey Henderson in 2006
d. Jimmy Campagna in 1952

158. Which player returned an interception 100 yards for a touchdown?

a. Larry West in 1972
b. Garry Moss in 1986
c. Steve Hughes in 1939
d. Charlie Britt in 1959

159. The school record for the longest kickoff return—99 yards—is shared by which two Georgia players?

a. Gene Washington and Kent Lawrence
b. Floyd Reid and Fred Gibson
c. Jimmy Campagna and Charley Trippi
d. Thomas Brown and Lindsay Scott

160. Who holds the record for most rushes (47) in a single game?

a. Herschel Walker in 1981
b. Charley Tripp in 1942
c. Garrison Hearst in 1992
d. Tim Worley in 1988

161. The record for most rushing touchdowns in a season (19) is held by _____.

a. Hershel Walker in 1981
b. Lars Tate in 1985
c. Tim Worley in 1988
d. Garrison Hearst in 1992

162. How many consecutive extra points did kicker Rex Robinson convert in his career for what was then the second-longest such streak in NCAA history?

a. 65
b. 83
c. 101
d. 154

163. Who is Georgia's all-time leading points scorer?

a. kicker Kevin Butler
b. running back Herschel Walker
c. quarterback Fran Tarkenton
d. quarterback/halfback Charley Trippi

164. How many Georgia records did quarterback Eric Zeier set in his college career?

a. 8
b. 16
c. 35
d. 67

OTHER COACHES

165. Robert Winston, Georgia's third coach, was the first one to _____.

a. be paid for the job
b. actively recruit players for the team
c. propose joining an athletic conference
d. appoint team captains

166. Winston was also notable for being _____.

a. deaf
b. a judge
c. a certified genius
d. English

167. Which American football legend was also an early Georgia head coach?

a. Pop Warner
b. Walter Camp
c. Amos Alonzo Stagg
d. Knute Rockne

168. Who was the first Georgia player to return as the team's head coach?

a. M.M. Dickinson
b. George Woodruff
c. Johnny Griffith
d. Wallace Butts

169. What did second coach Ernest Brown do during the 1883 season?

a. He introduced cheerleaders to the game day experience.
b. He introduced the forward pass to the Bulldog playbook.
c. He lined up at halfback during the Georgia Tech game.
d. He took the team on the road to an exhibition in Cuba.

170. Georgia player and Coach George Woodruff went by what nickname?

a. Tiny
b. Junior
c. Kid
d. Li'l George

171. Woodruff, already a wealthy businessman, received what annual salary for coaching the Bulldogs?

a. He did it for free.
b. $1
c. $100
d. $1,500

172. How many years did Wally Butts coach the Bulldogs?

a. 8
b. 12
c. 16
d. 21

173. Who replaced Vince Dooley as head coach?

a. Erskine Russell
b. Ray Goff
c. Jim Donnan
d. Mark Richt

IN THE PROS

174. Who was the first Georgia player taken in the 2008 NFL draft?

a. Thomas Brown
b. Chester Adams
c. Marcus Howard
d. Brandon Coutu

175. He was drafted by which team?

a. the Atlanta Falcons
b. the Chicago Bears
c. the Philadelphia Eagles
d. the Indianapolis Colts

176. The most Georgia players ever taken in a single NFL draft, as of 2008, were picked in 2002. How many Bulldogs were drafted?

a. 7
b. 8
c. 9
d. 10

177. Which Bulldog was the NFL's Most Valuable Player in 1998?

a. Garrison Hearst
b. Terrell Davis
c. Andre Hastings
d. Champ Bailey

178. Over the years, which NFL team has selected the most Bulldogs in the draft?

a. the Philadelphia Eagles
b. the San Francisco 49ers
c. the Green Bay Packers
d. the Denver Broncos

179. Georgia quarterback John Rauch later led which NFL team to a Super Bowl as head coach?

a. the Dallas Bowboys
b. the Chicago Bears
c. the Miami Dolphins
d. the Oakland Raiders

180. Which Bulldog was the first player selected overall in the 1953 NFL draft?

a. Harry Babcock
b. John Rauch
c. Zeke Bratkowski
d. Fran Tarkenton

181. How many seasons did quarterback Fran Tarkenton play in the NFL?

a. 8
b. 12
c. 15
d. 18

182. By the time of his retirement, how many career passing yards did Tarkenton have?

a. 5,003
b. 10,003
c. 23,003
d. 47,003

183. How many touchdowns (passing and rushing) did Tarkenton score as the back-up quarterback in his first game as a professional?

a. 3
b. 4
c. 5
d. 6

184. That game was also the first _____.

a. in the history of the Minnesota Vikings franchise
b. NFL game played on national television
c. night game played in the NFL
d. head-to-head meeting of an NFL and AFL team

185. Tarkenton was traded by the Vikings to the New York Giants in 1967 in exchange for _____.

a. all of the Giants' 1968 draft picks
b. Frank Gifford, Francis Peay, and Tucker Frederickson
c. Coach Allie Sherman and $500,000
d. two first-round and two second-round draft picks

186. Bulldog great Willie McClendon was drafted by which team in 1978?

a. the Green Bay Packers
b. the Chicago Bears
c. the Detroit Lions
d. the Minnesota Vikings

187. Jake Scott played nine seasons in the pros for which two teams?

a. the Miami Dolphins and the Washington Redskins
b. the Washington Redskins and the Baltimore Colts
c. the Philadelphia Eagles and the Detroit Lions
d. the Atlanta Falcons and the Dallas Cowboys

188. Who was the first Bulldog ever taken in the first round of the NFL draft?

a. Frank Sinkwich
b. Charley Trippi
c. Dan Edwards
d. Johnny Rauch

189. Garrison Hearst was drafted in the first round of the 1993 draft by which team?

a. the San Francisco 49ers
b. the Chicago Bears
c. the Arizona Cardinals
d. the Oakland Raiders

190. Clarence Kay, who went on to play nine seasons at tight end for the Denver Broncos, was originally selected in which round of the 1984 draft?

a. 1st
b. 2nd
c. 5th
d. 7th

191. Georgia tight end Troy Sadowski played 11 seasons in the NFL for _____ different teams.

a. 2
b. 4
c. 5
d. 7

192. Which two Bulldogs played on the Miami Dolphins' Super Bowl teams of the 1970s?

a. Royce Smith and Jake Scott
b. Jake Scott and Kent Lawrence
c. Jake Scott and Tommy Lyons
d. Bill Stanfill and Jake Scott

193. Which Bulldog quarterback took the Minnesota Vikings to the Super Bowl three times?

a. Larry Kohn
b. Matt Robinson
c. Fran Tarkenton
d. Larry Rakestraw

194. Charley Trippi helped lead which pro team to a championship in his rookie season?

a. the New York Yankees of the AAFC
b. the Chicago Bears
c. the Chicago Cardinals
d. the Green Bay Packers

195. Out of Georgia, Trippi was caught in a bidding war between the NFL and the All-America Football Conference and wound up signing a four-year deal for the then-massive sum of _____.

a. $5,000
b. $50,000
c. $100,000
d. $500,000

196. Which Georgia player did NOT go on to become a Super Bowl MVP?

a. Jake Scott
b. Terrell Davis
c. Hines Ward
d. Champ Bailey

197. All-American end Tom Nash later won three straight NFL championships with which team?

a. the Green Bay Packers
b. the Chicago Cardinals
c. the Detroit Lions
d. the Philadelphia Eagles

198. All-American offensive guard Edgar Chandler was later converted to what position in the NFL?

a. wide receiver
b. fullback
c. defensive tackle
d. linebacker

199. Center Tommy Lyons started how many consecutive games in the NFL with the Denver Broncos before breaking his leg in 1975?

a. 33
b. 49
c. 54
d. 68

200. While he was in the NFL, Lyons also _____.

a. finished his undergraduate degree at Georgia
b. passed the Bar
c. earned his medical degree
d. completed a PhD in psychology

ANSWERS

1. b)	22. a)	43. d)	64. b)
2. a)	23. b)	44. c)	65. c)
3. d)	24. c)	45. b)	66. a)
4. a)	25. b)	46. d)	67. a)
5. c)	26. c)	47. c)	68. c)
6. a)	27. b)	48. d)	69. a)
7. d)	28. a)	49. a)	70. d)
8. c)	29. d)	50. d)	71. d)
9. b)	30. a)	51. b)	72. a)
10. c)	31. b)	52. b)	73. a)
11. b)	32. a)	53. b)	74. b)
12. a)	33. a)	54. c)	75. b)
13. d)	34. b)	55. c)	76. a)
14. a)	35. c)	56. d)	77. d)
15. d)	36. b)	57. d)	78. b)
16. c)	37. c)	58. b)	79. d)
17. d)	38. c)	59. d)	80. a)
18. a)	39. c)	60. a)	81. d)
19. b)	40. c)	61. c)	82. b)
20. c)	41. b)	62. c)	83. d)
21. d)	42. c)	63. c)	84. b)

85. c)	114. b)	143. c)	172. d)
86. c)	115. a)	144. a)	173. b)
87. b)	116. a)	145. b)	174. c)
88. a)	117. c)	146. a)	175. d)
89. d)	118. c)	147. c)	176. b)
90. c)	119. c)	148. d)	177. b)
91. b)	120. a)	149. c)	178. a)
92. b)	121. d)	150. c)	179. d)
93. b)	122. c)	151. c)	180. a)
94. d)	123. a)	152. d)	181. d)
95. d)	124. b)	153. b)	182. d)
96. c)	125. a)	154. c)	183. c)
97. a)	126. d)	155. b)	184. a)
98. d)	127. b)	156. c)	185. d)
99. b)	128. b)	157. d)	186. b)
100. a)	129. c)	158. d)	187. a)
101. d)	130. a)	159. d)	188. a)
102. b)	131. d)	160. a)	189. c)
103. c)	132. c)	161. d)	190. d)
104. d)	133. c)	162. c)	191. d)
105. c)	134. b)	163. a)	192. d)
106. a)	135. b)	164. d)	193. c)
107. c)	136. b)	165. a)	194. c)
108. b)	137. a)	166. d)	195. c)
109. a)	138. d)	167. a)	196. d)
110. d)	139. b)	168. a)	197. a)
111. c)	140. c)	169. c)	198. d)
112. b)	141. d)	170. c)	199. b)
113. c)	142. d)	171. b)	200. c)